Editor
Mara Ellen Guckian

Managing Editor
Ina Massler Levin, M.A.

Editor-in-Chief
Sharon Coan, M.S. Ed.

Illustrators
Ken Tunell
Victoria Ponikvar-Frazier
Bruce Hedges

Art Coordinator
Denice Adorno

Cover Design
Denice Adorno

Imaging
Ralph Olmedo Jr.
James Edward Grace
Rosa C. See
Alfred Lau

Production Manager
Phil Garcia

Publishers
Rachelle Cracchiolo, M.S. Ed.
Mary Dupuy Smith, M.S. Ed.

SOCIAL STUDIES UNITS

with Reproducible

Little Books

Can I help?
Rake the
leaves.

Authors

Renee Chauncey, Ed. S.
Tammy Girtman, Ed. S.

Teacher Created Materials, Inc.
6421 Industry Way
Westminster, CA 92683
www.teachercreated.com
ISBN-1-7439-3252-8
©2001 Teacher Created Materials, Inc.
Made in U.S.A.

Table of Contents

Introduction

Social Studies Units with Reproducible Little Books creates a unique opportunity for children. Teaching children about social studies concepts provides a way to make children aware of the world around them. Social studies concepts allow children to experience how families, communities, and society in general work together.

The units contain mini-book readers that are an excellent source for building confidence in a child's reading ability. Each concept has a mini-book reader that has phonetically decodable words and sight words to challenge and build fluency in young, emergent readers. The mini-books are comprised of facts and terms relevant to the concept being studied. Mini-books can be incorporated in repeated readings, choral reading, shared reading, and echo reading. The patterns offer additional opportunities to explore the topics being discussed. They can be enlarged to suit class needs.

Fun page activities are designed to allow the teacher to pick and choose activities that meet the needs of the classroom and personal teaching style. The fun page contains: brief facts, activities, related books, and websites.

The book lists offer both factual and fictional literature that will pique the students' interest in each concept. Activities are included to incorporate problem solving and critical thinking skills into exciting challenges for the children. Art projects are provided to bring each concept to life. The hands-on creations allow the children meaningful and authentic learning through the application of color, texture, and design of each concept.

The websites can be used as a navigational tool for research projects, reports, teacher information, and visual imagery of the concept. When visiting the sites, please click on or type in the subject area to be studied and follow the links. At the time of publication, these sites were active. If they are no longer active, go to a search engine such as google.com. Try typing in key words related to your topic. In most cases the unit title will work.

The final section of the book has journal pages for each topic. Journal writing activities allow children to reflect upon what they are learning and what they enjoy about each concept. Children will be excited to express their thoughts about each concept while providing the opportunity to practice connecting the letter/sound relationship of words.

Introduction (cont.)

Using this unit incorporates the following:

Social Studies Vocabulary—The student will learn new vocabulary words relating to the topic that the class is studying at the time.

Sight Word Usage—The student will increase his or her sight word vocabulary through learning to read the mini books.

Shared Reading Opportunities—The student will be able to read the mini books for each individual unit to a special friend.

Choral Reading—Because the whole class will be learning to read the same books, each student will be able to read the mini book with one or more friends.

Echo Reading—Because the books are written in pattern form, it is easy for the teacher to help the student learn to read the book through echo reading. The teacher says the line first and the student echos the line back.

Journal Reading—The teacher is encouraged to provide multiple opportunities for the student to write.

Authentic Literature—A list of corresponding literature is provided at the beginning of each unit.

Technology Connections—A list of corresponding Web sites is provided at the beginning of each unit.

Art Projects—Each unit provides suggestions for art projects that will encourage the students' creativity.

Opportunities to Observe/Investigate, and Reflect —Each unit provides opportunities for students to increase their knowledge of the world around them.

User Friendliness—The individual units are organized in a way that they can be used consecutively or at different times throughout the year. The units are short but contain a wealth of information for the young student to absorb.

The following is an example of how to set up a lesson using this unit.

1. Choose a book from the book list or choose one of your favorites.

2. Identify the concept that will be studied.

3. Make a class list of known facts about the concept.

4. Read a mini book.

5. Search the Internet (URLs are listed).

6. Choose one or more of the suggested fun activities.

7. Construct an art project. Arrange an area to display finished work.

8. End with journal writing.

Who works in our community?

1) Nurses
2) Police Officers
3) Crossing Guards
4) Doctors
5) Librarians

Helpful Hints

Art Hints

- Practice *tracing* on lines with the children. Explain that they are to draw right on the lines of the picture.

- If the project calls for *watercolor* paint, you may add water to tempera paint.

- If the project calls for a *paper headband*, try using a sentence strip or a 9"x 12" sheet of construction paper cut lengthwise. Size the strip to each child's head and staple it together.

Journal Writing Hints

There are several ways to incorporate journal writing into a unit of study. Two suggestions are listed below.

1. Copy the journal pages and combine them into one book by stapling or binding them together. Children may use this journal to write facts about each topic, or as a creative writing tool.

2. The journal pages may also be used individually with each topic and then bound together at the end of the study.

Internet Sites

When visiting the sites please click on or type in the subject area to be studied and follow the links.

Mini Book Reader

Use the following steps to put together a mini-book reader.

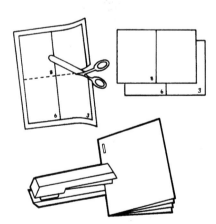

1. Make a two-sided copy of the mini-book pages.

2. Cut the two-sided page in half horizontally on the dashed line.

3. Place mini-book pages 6 and 3 behind page 8 and the title page. Double check that the pages are all facing up and that they are in order.

4. Fold the pages and staple them on the fold.

Note: If a two-sided copy of the mini book is not available, use these steps to put the minibook together.

1. Cut out the mini-book pages.

2. Place the pages in numerical order starting with the title page and ending with page eight.

3. Staple the pages together on the top left corner or along the left side.

Family Fun

Family Facts

- Everyone is part of a family.
- Families change.
- Families spend time together at home.
- Families eat, sleep and play together.
- Families make choices together.
- Families have responsibilities.
- Families have fun together.
- All families are different.
- Families help one another.
- There are many family members: dad, mom, sister, brother, aunt, uncle, grandmother, grandfather, etc.
- Some families have step-parents, step-brothers, step-sisters, etc.

Family Fun Activities

1. Draw a picture of your family.
2. Have children bring pictures of themselves and their families.
3. Keep a family journal. Write about things done together as a family.
4. Graph the number of people in each child's family.
5. Discuss chores that are done at home to help the family.
6. Invite each child's family to eat lunch with the class.

Book List

Eastman, P.D. *Are You My Mother?* Random House, Inc., 1998.

Maclachan, Patricia. *Through Grandpa's Eyes.* Harper Collins, 1983.

Munsch, Robert. *Love You Forever.* Firefly Books Ltd., 1998.

Pellegrini, Nina. *Families are Different.* Holiday, 1991.

Penn, Audrey. *The Kissing Hand.* Child Welfare League of America, Inc. 1995.

Rylant, Cynthia. *The Relatives Came.* Simon & Schuster, 1993.

Family Sites

http://www.alfy.com/teachers/index.asp
This site is full of thematic units! Click on "more thematic units." The families' unit contains stories about families.

http://www.track0.com/canteach
Let your children experience songs and poems about families with this fun site. Just click on "songs and poems" and then "families."

http://www.childfun.com
Child Fun contains activities, songs, and poems about families.

http://www.carolhurst.com/newsletters/23bnewsletters.html
This site offers a great teacher resource guide for teaching the concept of families.

How can you help?

8

A Family Helps

Can I Help?

Rake the leaves.

6

Can I Help?

Mow the lawn.

3

Can I help?

Wash the dishes.

2

Can I help?

Feed the pets.

7

Can I help?

Do the laundry.

4

Can I help?

Plant the garden.

5

You are part of the family.

A Family

(draw yourself)

8

A grandpa is part of a family.

6

A mom is part of a family.

3

A dad is part of a family.

2

A grandma is part of a family.

7

A sister is part of a family.

4

A brother is part of a family.

5

Family Pattern

House

Teacher Directions: Copy the pattern onto white construction paper.

- -

Directions:

1. Color and cut out the house pattern.

2. Cut the door on the dashed lines.

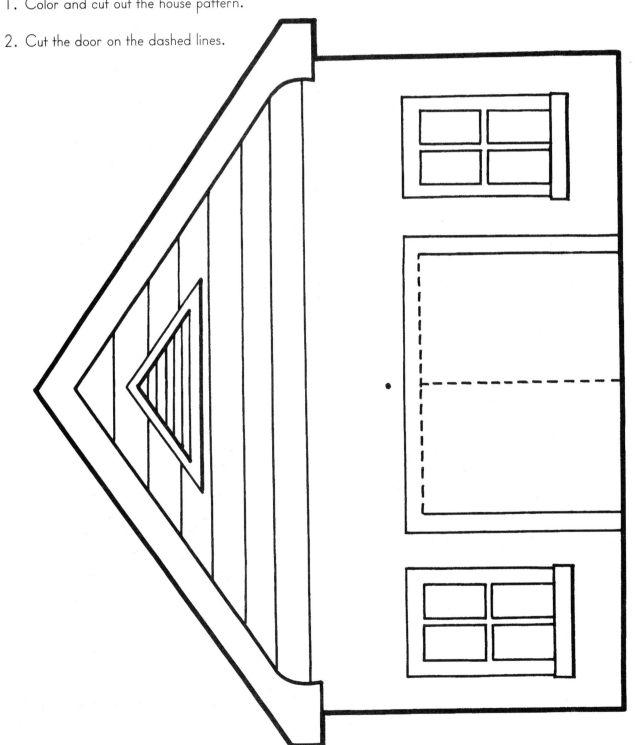

Family Pattern

Wheel

Teacher Directions: Copy the pattern onto white construction paper. Use with page 11.

- -

Directions:

1. Color and cut out the wheel pattern.

2. Draw a family member in each section. Label the family member.

3. Attach the wheel pattern to the back of the house, using a paper fastener.

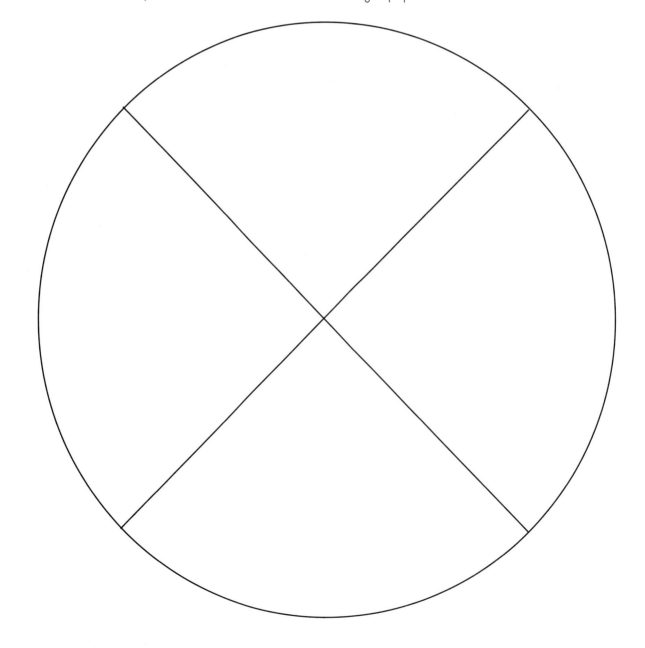

Different Homes Fun

Different Homes Facts

- A home is a place where people eat, sleep, and play together.
- Everyone needs a home.
- There are many kinds of homes.
- Homes are different shapes and sizes.
- Homes are for people and for animals.
- A long time ago, people built homes from local materials.
- Homes can be made of wood, stone, grass, mud, and ice, etc.
- Some homes can be moved easily such as tents, houseboats, and homes on wheels.
- Homes keep us safe from the things in our environment including wild animals and different weather conditions.
- An apartment building has many homes.

Different Homes Fun Activities

1. Draw a picture of your home.
2. Graph the different kinds of homes represented in the class.
3. Design a futuristic home using various art supplies: craft sticks, boxes, buttons, colored cellophane, etc.
4. List the different materials that can be used to build a home.
5. Compare and contrast homes of today to homes of long ago.
6. Locate pictures of different homes found in magazines— cut out the pictures and make a collage.

Book List

Feder, Paula. *Where Does the Teacher Live?* E. P. Dutton, 1999.

Jackson, Mike. *Homes Around the World.* Raintree Steck-Vaughn Publishers, 1995.

Kalman, Bobbie. *Homes Around the World.* Crabtree Publishing Company, 1994.

Morris, Ann. *Homes and Homes.* William Morrow & Co., 1995.

Different Homes Sites

http://www.kstrom.net/isk/maps/houses/igloo.html
Check out some interesting information about the history of igloos and how they are built.

http://architecture.about.com/arts/architecture/library/weekly/aa050700a.htm
Find out how the environment influences the structure of some houses. This site has great pictures of grass houses, pueblos and homes built into the earth.

http://www.galleriacollection.com/coffee/coffee2.htm
Visit a small village of grass huts.

a home is a place where people live.

8

Homes

Apartment

Big or small

6

Mobile Home

A home can be on wheels

3

A home is where people live.

2

round or square,

7

or on stilts.

4

A home is where people live.

5

15

Different Homes Pattern
Houseboat Cabin

Teacher Directions: Copy the pattern onto white construction paper. Use with page 17.

Directions:

1. Color and cut out the houseboat cabin pattern.

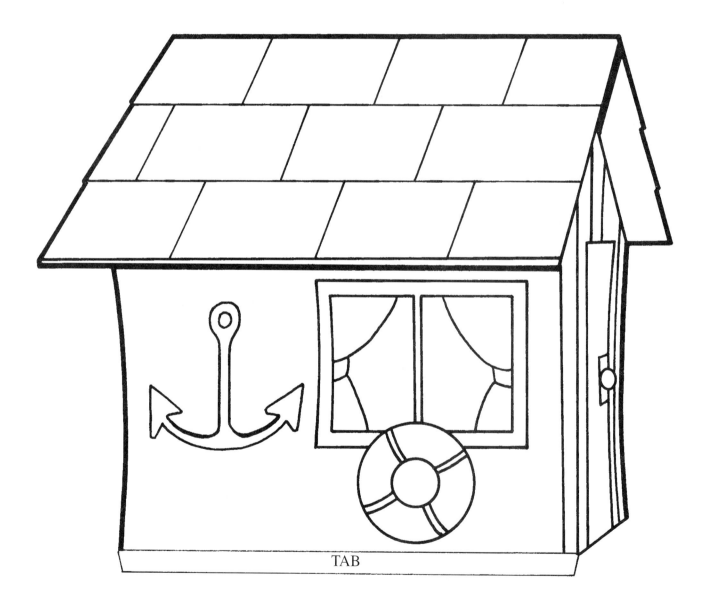

Different Homes Pattern

Houseboat Bottom

Teacher Directions: Copy the pattern onto white construction paper. Use with page 16.

Directions

1. Trace over the lines of the boat using a brown crayon.

2. Paint the boat using brown watercolor.

3. Cut out the boat pattern.

4. Attach the boat to the cabin pattern.

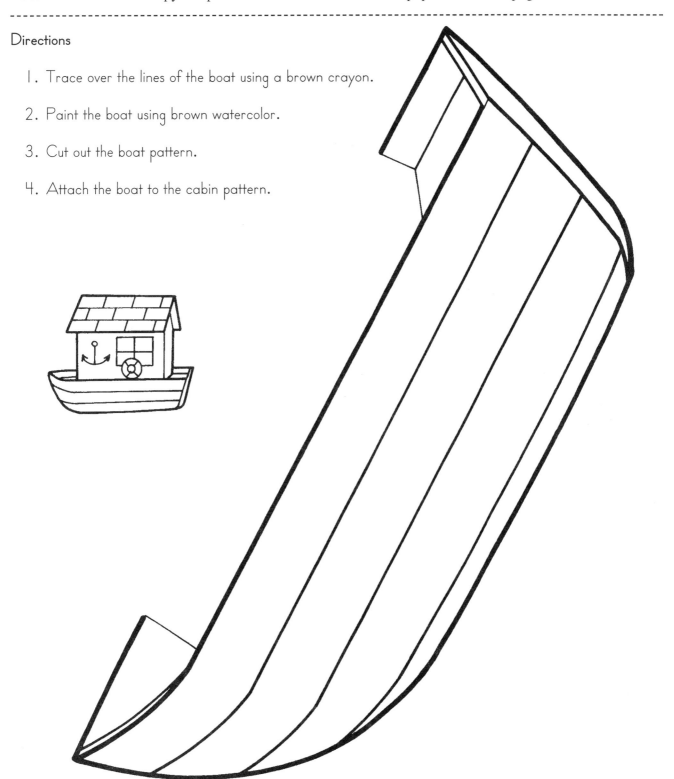

Different Homes Pattern

Grass Hut Roof

Teacher Directions: Copy the pattern onto white construction paper. Use with page 19.

- -

Directions

1. Tear brown construction paper into strips.

2. Glue the strips to the pattern.

3. Cut out the pattern.

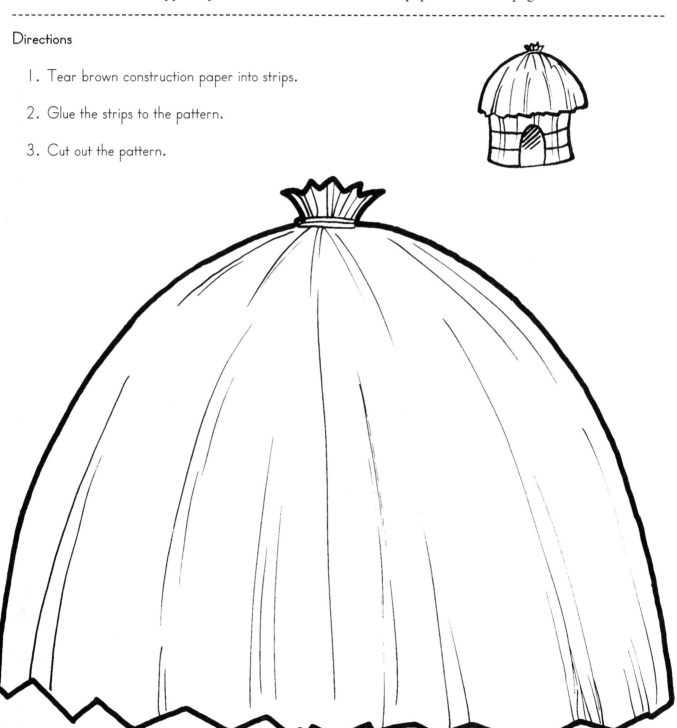

Different Homes Pattern

Grass Hut Bottom

Teacher Directions: Copy the pattern onto white construction paper. Use with page 18.

Directions

1. Use a black crayon to trace over the lines of the pattern.

2. Paint the hut using brown watercolor.

3. Cut out the hut pattern.

4. Attach to the hut roof pattern.

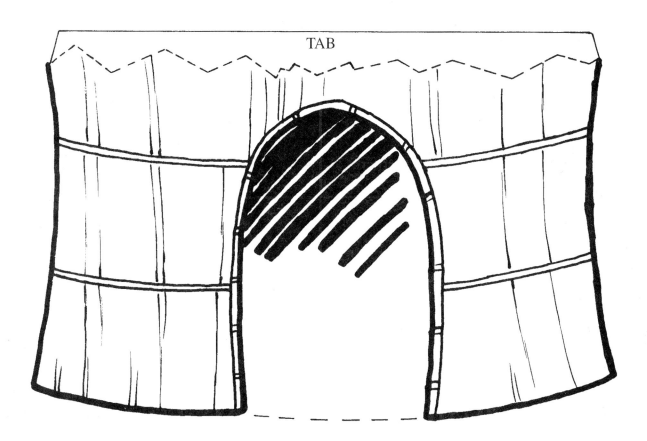

School Fun

School Facts

- School is a place for learning.
- A school is part of the community.
- Schools have workers.
- Teachers help children learn.
- A principal is in charge of the school.
- A school has rules to keep children safe.
- The media specialist helps children find interesting books.
- The custodians help keep the school clean.
- A student's job is to learn.
- A school has tools to help children learn—books, computers, rulers, manipulatives, etc.

School Fun Activities

1. Draw a map of your school.
2. Write thank you notes to the people who work in the school.
3. Draw a picture and write about what you like best about school.
4. Research and find out the history about your school. How long has it been in existence? Who is it named for and why?
5. Invite the principal to read a story to the class.
6. Help keep the playground clean. Have a trash pick-up day every week.

Book List

Cazet, Denys. *Never Spit on Your Shoes.* Orchard Books, 1993.

Henkes, Kevin. *Chrysanthemum.* Morrow, William & Co., 1996.

London, Jonathan. *Froggy Goes to School.* Penguin Putnam Books for Young Readers, 1998.

Penn, Audrey. *The Kissing Hand.* Child Welfare League of America, Inc., 1995.

School Sites

http://www.gushers.com/
This is a fun site for kids. Children choose a locker number and enter school. This site is full of games.

http://www.enchantedlearning.com/Home.html
The Enchanted Learning site is a wonderful resource for teachers and students. This site is easy to read and informative.

http://www.epals.com
Join epals and communicate with other classes and the world.

These are my friends.

8

My School

This is my teacher.

6

This is my school.

3

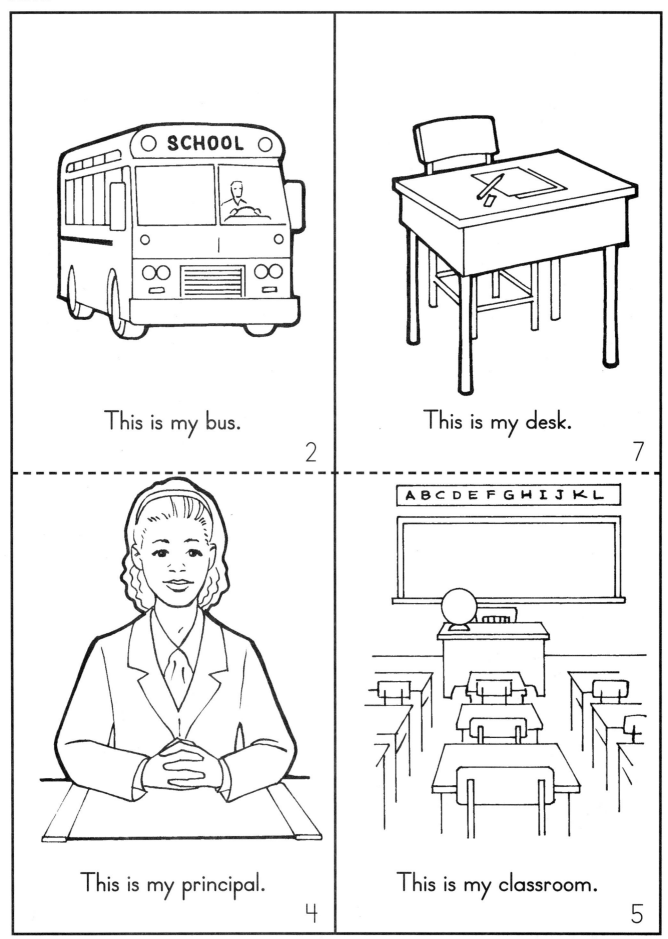

This is my bus.

2

This is my desk.

7

This is my principal.

4

This is my classroom.

5

I like to learn about the world.

8

School Fun

I like to read.

6

I have fun at school.

3

My name is Jeff.

2

I like to learn about numbers.

7

I like to paint.

4

I like to play with my friends.

5

School Pattern

Child's Head

Teacher Directions: Copy the pattern onto white construction paper. Use with pages 26, 27, and 28.

- -

Directions

1. Draw your face on the pattern.

2. Cut the pattern out.

3. Attach construction paper strips or yarn to the head to make hair.

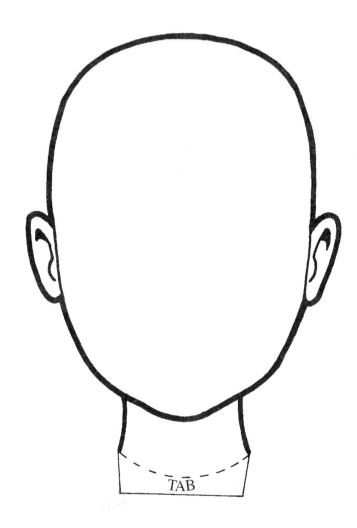

TAB

School Pattern

Shirt

Teacher Directions: Copy the pattern onto white construction paper. (School colors are cute for this project.) Use with pages 25, 27, and 28.

Directions

1. Decorate and color the shirt pattern.

2. Cut out the pattern.

3. Attach the shirt to the head pattern.

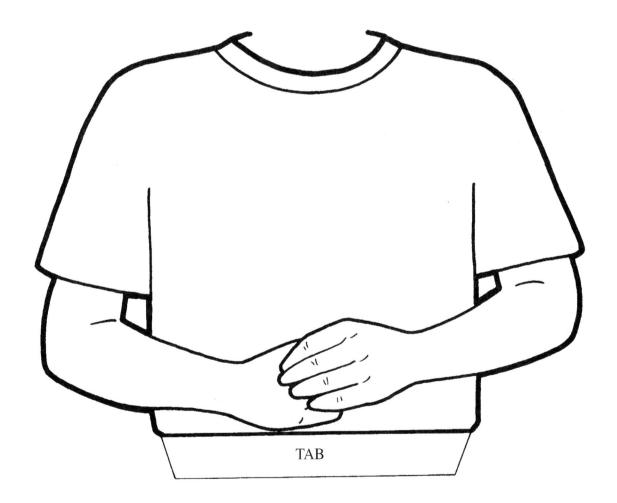

TAB

School Pattern

Boy

Teacher Directions: Copy the pattern onto white construction paper. Use with pages 25 and 26.

- -

Directions

1. Color the pattern.

2. Cut out the pattern.

3. Attach to the shirt pattern.

School Pattern

Girl

Teacher Directions: Copy the pattern onto white construction paper. Use with pages 25 and 26.

Directions

1. Color the pattern.

2. Cut out the pattern.

3. Attach to the shirt pattern.

Community Helpers Fun

Community Helpers Facts

- A community is a place where people live, work and play.
- People who work in the community are community helpers.
- Community helpers provide services that help people.
- A police officer protects you and your community.
- A fire fighter keeps you and your community safe from fires.
- A banker works in a bank where people keep their money.
- A hospital is a place in the community where people go when they are sick.
- Doctors and nurses work in the community to help keep people well.
- A post office is a place where mail is picked up, sorted, and delivered to your community and around the world.
- A community offers many different jobs.

Community Helpers Activities

1. Invite different community helpers to visit your classroom and discuss their jobs.
2. Go on field trips to different places in your community.
3. Write a letter to a friend or family member and mail it at the post office.
4. Encourage parents to take their children to the bank and discuss what transactions take place at a bank.
5. Make a class graph depicting what each child wants to be when he or she grows up.
6. Draw a fire escape plan showing at least two ways out of the house or classroom.

Book List

Baseball Player – Noah

Bryant-Mole, Karen. *You're a Community Helper.* Heinemann, 1998.

Kalman, Bobbie. *Community Helpers from A to Z.* Crabtree Publishing Company, 1999.

Kalman, Bobbie. *People at Work.* Crabtree Publishing Company, 1986.

Kottke, Jan. *A Day with Police Officers.* Children's Press, 2000.

Community Helper Sites

http://www.beenleigss.qld.edu.au/requested_sites/services
This Community Helpers site asks question about different community helpers. Links are provided to research the answers.

http://www.whatdotheydo.com
Explore different community helpers that can be found in your community. Find out about community helpers from A-Z.

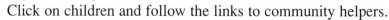

http://www.ncpc.org/10act10.htm
Test your community helper knowledge in this hidden answer quiz. Picture icons are used to match the answers.

http://www.kirksvillecity.com/fire/safety
Learn about fire safety.

http://www.kidsbank.com/index.html
Kids Bank explores how money is made, how to save money, and how to write checks.

http://www.ncpc.com
Click on children and follow the links to community helpers.

Who works in your community?

Community Helpers

HOSPITAL

Post Office

Fire Station

POLICE

8

Who works in a community?

Who works in a community?

a fire fighter

6

a doctor

3

Who works in a community?

a postal worker

2

Who works in a community?

a banker

7

Who works in a community?

a nurse

4

Who works in a community?

a police officer

5

My friend smiles when he reads his letter.

8

The Post Office

A big machine sorts the mail.

6

Dear Friend,

I miss you.

I write him letters to keep in touch.

3

I have a friend who lives far away. I miss him a lot.

2

It is flown from here to there.

7

I put the letter in an envelope. I put a stamp on it. I put it in my mailbox.

4

The mail carrier takes it to the post office.

5

Post Office Pattern

Mail Carrier

Teacher Directions: Copy the pattern onto white construction paper. Use with page 35.

Directions

1. Color and cut out the patterns.

2. Attach the mail bag, letters and head to the body pattern.

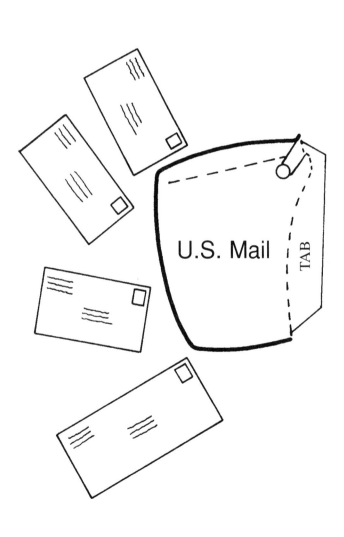

Post Office Pattern

Mail Carrier Body

Teacher Directions: Copy the pattern onto white construction paper. Use with page 34.

Directions

1. Color the pattern.

2. Cut out the pattern.

3. Attach the body pattern to the head pattern.

Guess what I told about for show and tell?

8

Hospital

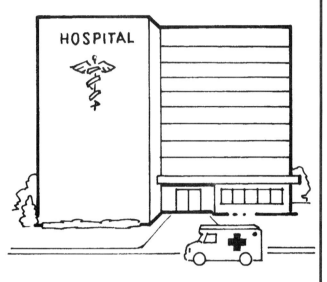

HOSPITAL

It's broken!

The doctor put a cast on my leg.

6

One day I had an accident.

3

I have a favorite tree that I love to climb.

2

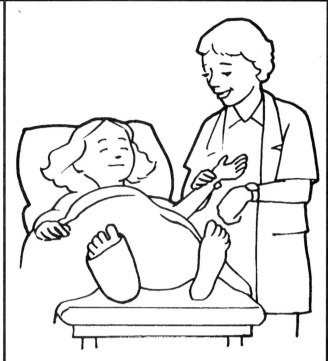

The doctors and nurses at the hospital took good care of me.

7

An ambulance took me to the hospital.

4

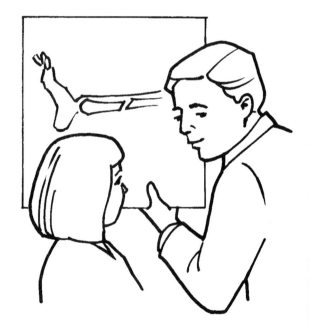

A nurse took me to have an xray.

5

Hospital Pattern

Doctor

Teacher Directions: Copy the pattern onto white construction paper. Use with page 39.

Directions

Color and cut out the pattern.

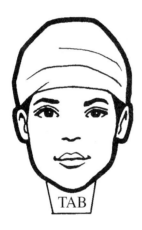

Hospital Pattern

Doctor's Body

Teacher Directions: Copy the pattern onto white construction paper. Use with page 38.

Directions

1. Color and cut out the pattern.

2. Attach the body pattern to the head pattern.

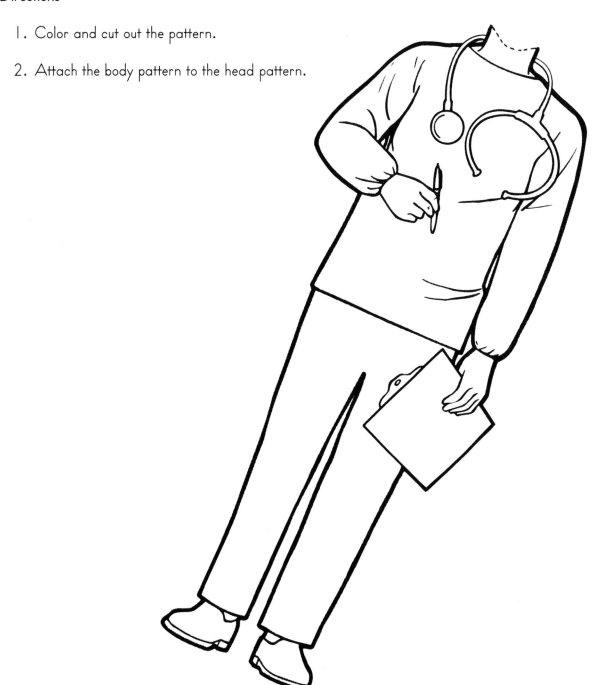

I have saved enough money to buy a new bike!

8

The Bank

She gives me a savings book.

6

My mom says I need to put my money in the bank.

3

I am working to earn money. I want to buy something great!

2

She puts my money in a vault.

7

This is the bank where my mom puts her money. They will keep it safe.

4

This is a teller. She counts my money.

5

Bank Pattern

Teller

Teacher Directions: Copy the pattern onto white construction paper. Use with page 43.

- -

Directions

1. Color the patterns.

2. Cut out the patterns.

Bank Pattern

Teller's Body

Teacher Directions: Copy the pattern onto white construction paper. Use with page 42.

Directions

1. Color the pattern.

2. Cut out the pattern.

3. Attach the body pattern to the head pattern.

4. Attach the money and money bag.

Police officers are our friends.

8

Police

A police officer protects people.

6

A police officer is a community helper.

3

This is a police officer.

2

A police officer has many jobs.

4

A police officer reminds us to follow the law.

7

A police officer directs traffic.

5

Police Officer Pattern

Officer and Dog

Teacher Directions: Copy the pattern onto white construction paper. Use with page 47.

Directions

Color and cut out the patterns.

Police Officer Pattern

Officer's Body

Teacher Directions: Copy the pattern onto white construction paper. Use with page 46.

- -

Directions

1. Color and cut out the pattern.

2. Glue pattern over the tab of the head pattern.

3. Attach the flashlight.

Fire fighters are our friends.

8

Fire Fighters

A fire fighter puts out fires.

6

A fire fighter is a community helper.

3

This is a fire fighter.

2

Fire fighters use fire trucks to help put out fires.

7

A fire fighter has special clothes.

4

A fire fighter has special tools.

5

Fire Fighter Pattern

Fire Fighter and Extinguisher

Teacher Directions: Copy the pattern onto white construction paper. Use with page 51.

Directions

1. Color and cut out the pattern.

2. Attach the head to the body.

Fire Fighter Pattern

Fire Fighter's Body

Teacher Directions: Copy the pattern onto white construction paper. Use with page 50.

Directions

1. Color and cut out the pattern.

2. Attach the pattern to the head pattern.

3. Glue the fire extinguisher

    to the fire fighter's hand.

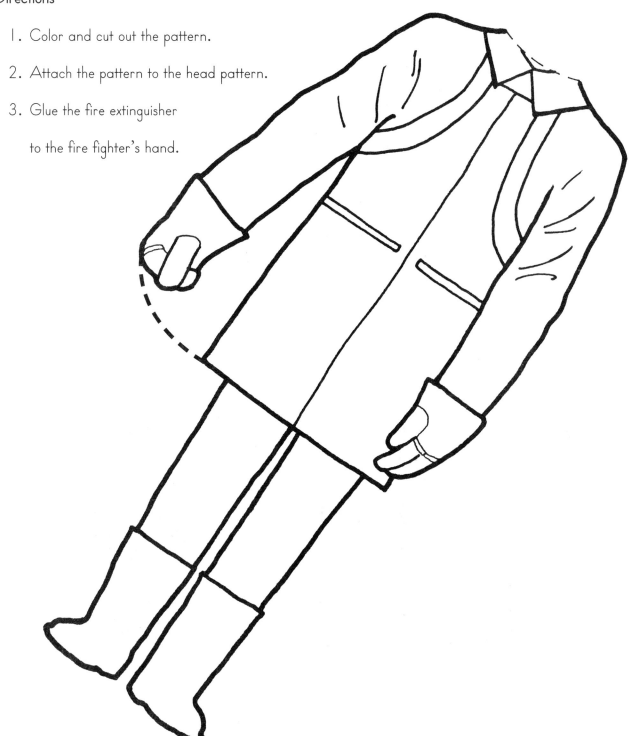

Producer to Consumer Fun

Producer to Consumer Facts

- A producer is someone who grows or makes something to be sold.
- A farmer is a producer.
- A consumer is someone who buys goods.
- Goods are something that have been produced (food, clothing, toys, etc.).
- A factory is a place where workers process resources into goods.
- Factories have special machines to process "goods."
- Factories sell goods to markets or stores.
- Trucks transport goods from the factory to the markets and stores.
- People shop at the market or stores to buy "goods" they need.

Producer to Consumer Fun Activities

1. Visit a farm and find out what is produced there.
2. Tour a factory. Learn about what they make and where it goes.
3. Go on a scavenger hunt at a local store and identify products made from milk.
4. Have a tasting party of dairy foods. Be sure to include things like cottage cheese, yogurt, etc.
5. Graph your favorite milk products.

Book List

Gibbons, Gail. *The Milk Makers.* Aladdin Paperbacks, 1987.

Kalman, Bobbie. *Hurray for Dairy Farming!* Crabtree Publishing, 1997.

Peterson, Cris. *Extra Cheese, Please!: Mozzarella's Journey from Cow to Pizza.* Boyds Mills, 1994.

Sloat, Teri. *Farmer Brown Sheers His Sheep.* DK Publishing, 2000.

Producer to Consumer Sites

http://tqjunior.thinkquest.org/3901
The Econopolis site gives a brief, easy-to-understand definition of producer, consumer, goods, services, and supply and demand.

http://www.got-milk.com
Where does milk come from? This site gives you interesting information about the process of getting milk.

http://www.moomilk.com
Take a virtual tour of the "Milk Story."

http://www.idahoforests.org/kids1.htm
Visit the Idaho Forests Kid's site to discover products that come from trees and learn how paper is made.

Producer to Consumer

Which milk product do you like best?

8

Milk is used to make cheese.

6

Farmer Moo milks Daisy.

3

This is Farmer Moo and his dairy cow, Daisy.

2

Milk is used to make butter and other dairy products.

7

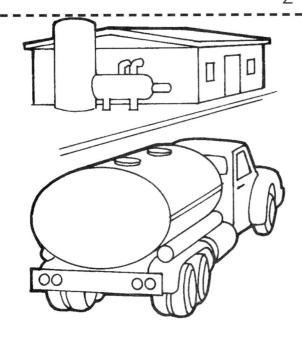

A special truck takes the milk to a factory.

4

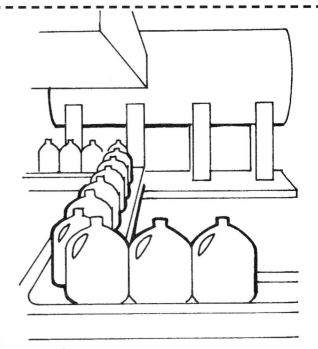

Special machines are used to get the milk ready for people to use.

5

What is made from a tree?

8

Producer to Consumer: Trees

Big trucks take the trees to the lumber yard.

6

She has a tree farm.

3

This is Farmer Green.

2

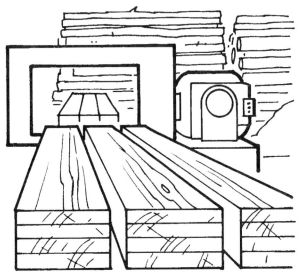

Special machines are used to change the trees into products people use.

7

She takes special care of the trees.

4

Farmer Green uses special machines to cut the trees.

5

Producer to Consumer Pattern

Cow's Head

Teacher Directions: Copy the pattern onto white construction paper. Use with pages 58, 59, and 60.

- -

Directions

1. Color the cow's spots black.

2. Cut out the pattern.

Producer to Consumer Pattern

Cow's Body

Teacher Directions: Copy the pattern onto white construction paper. Use with pages 57, 59, and 60.

Directions

1. Color the cow's spots black.

2. Cut out the pattern.

3. Attach the body to the head.

Producer to Consumer Pattern

Cow's Tail and Legs

Teacher Directions: Copy the pattern onto white construction paper. Use with pages 57, 58, and 60.

Directions

1. Color the hooves and spots black.

2. Cut out the patterns.

3. Glue to the cow body pattern.

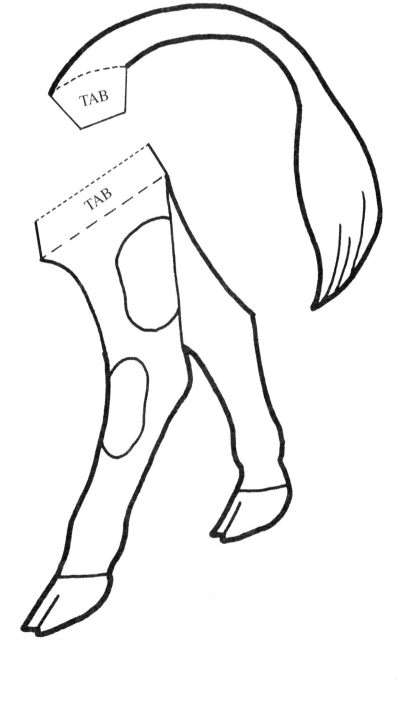

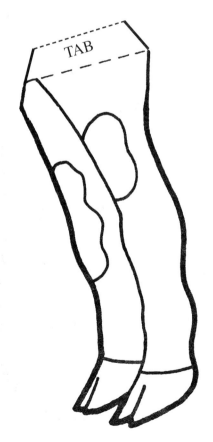

Producer to Consumer Pattern

Dairy Products

Teacher Directions: Copy the pattern onto white construction paper. Each child needs 4-12 inch pieces of yarn. Use with pages 57, 58, and 59.

- -

Directions

1. Color the patterns.

2. Cut out the patterns.

3. Tape one piece of yarn to the top of each dairy product.

4. Tape the other end of the yarn to the bottom of the cow's body.

Transportation Fun

Transportation Facts

- Transportation is the way people and goods get from one place to another.
- People are working to invent new and better ways of transportation.
- Long ago transportation was quite different from what we have today.
- Some methods of transportation from long ago include horses, buggies, trains, boats, canoes, etc.
- Some methods of transportation today include cars, trains, airplanes, helicopters, space shuttles, ships, etc.
- Today's transportation allows people to get from one place to another quickly.
- Some people get special training to drive certain types of transportation (pilots, train conductors, boat captains, etc.).

Transportation Activities

1. Draw pictures and discuss the ways you have traveled.
2. Draw a picture of how transportation will look in the future.
3. Locate pictures in magazines to represent different modes of transportation. Try to find pictures of transportation vehicles from long ago and compare them.
4. Go on a field trip to an airport, train station, or bus station.
5. Graph how you travel to school.
6. Research to find out how fast your favorite mode of transportation can travel.

Book List

Fradin, Dennis. *Transportation: Helicopters.* Children's Press, 1997.

Yaccarino, Dan. *Zoom Zoom Zoom I'm Off to the Moon.* Scholastic Trade, 1997.

Transportation Sites

http://www.balloonfiesta.com/edu/index.htm
Learn about hot air balloons and how they work from the Albuquerque International Balloon Festival.

http://www.transitpeople.org/lesson/trancovr.htm
Do you know who invented the train or the automobile?
The Transit People site gives a brief overview of the development of transportation.

http://spacelink.nasa.gov/.index.html
Explore the galaxy with the NASA site. Learn about the space shuttle and space travel.

http://cbc4kids.ca/general/the-lab/history-of-invention
Investigate the time line of inventions.

How do you get from here to there?

How Do We Get From Here to There?

(draw yourself)

8

How do we get from here to there?

a train

6

How do we get from here to there?

a bus

3

How do we get from here to there?

a car

2

How do we get from here to there?

a subway

7

How do we get from here to there?

a boat

4

How do we get from here to there?

an airplane

5

When you grow up what will you choose?

8

Traffic

Motorcycles, bicycles,

6

Cars and trucks everywhere— trying to get from here to there.

3

64

Toot-toot,

    honk-honk,

        beep-beep...

2

4-wheelers too!
They make driving fun for me and you.

7

Stuck in traffic,
they can't move.

4

It's a jam. What can they do?

5

Transportation Pattern

Truck Cab

Teacher Directions: Copy the pattern onto white construction paper. Use with page 67.

Directions

1. Color the cab.

2. Cut the cab pattern out.

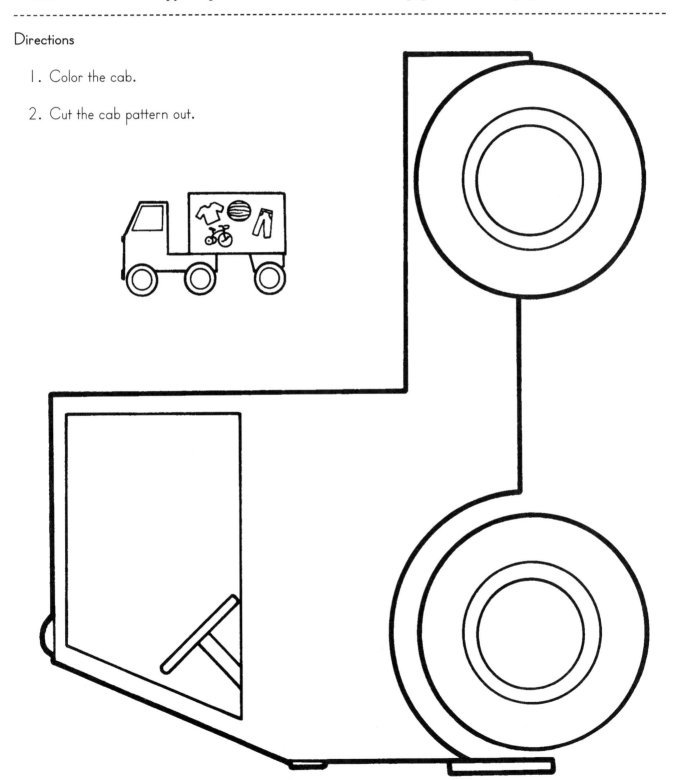

Transportation Pattern

Truck Trailer

Teacher Directions: Copy the pattern onto white construction paper. Provide magazines for students. Use with page 66.

Directions

1. Color the trailer.

2. Find and cut out pictures of "goods" that can be hauled in the trailer.

3. Cut the pattern out and glue it to the cab.

4. Glue the pictures to the trailer.

TAB

Flying is one way to get from here to there.

8

Air Transportation

3

Zooming...

6

I want to be part of the world out there.

3

Soaring, turning, gliding, and floating, through the air . . .

2

Soaring through the air.

7

Floating...

4

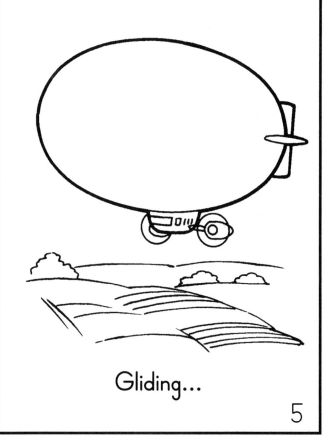

Gliding...

5

Air Transportation Pattern

Hot Air Balloon

Teacher Directions: Copy the pattern onto white construction paper. Use with page 71.

Directions

1. Cut the pattern out.

2. Decorate the balloon by gluing different colored pieces of torn construction paper to it.

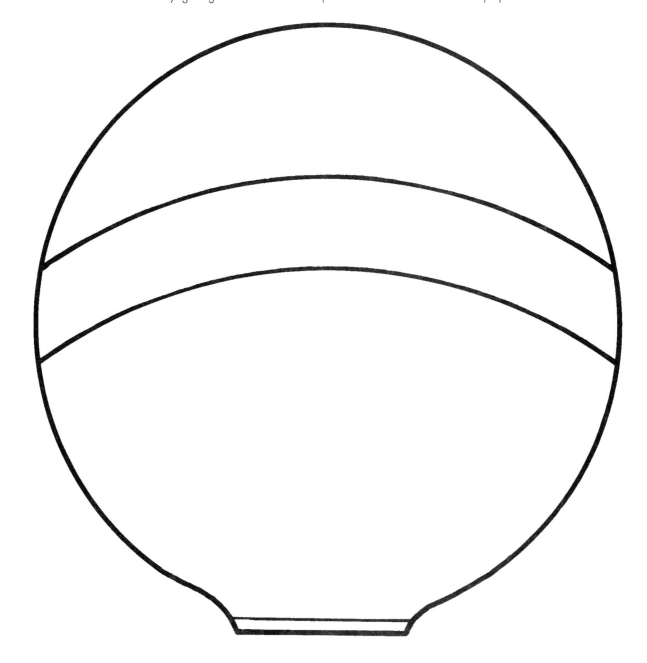

Air Transportation Pattern

Hot Air Balloon Basket

Teacher Directions: Copy the pattern onto white construction paper. Each child will need two 6"
pieces of yarn. Use with page 70.

Directions

1. Color the children in the basket.

2. Trace over the lines of the basket using a brown crayon.

3. Paint the basket, using brown watercolor.

4. Cut the pattern out.

5. Attach the balloon to the basket using yarn and tape.

...and wave to everyone I pass.

8

A Train

I would like to climb aboard
and make the train go fast.

6

Here comes a train chugging
down the tracks.

3

Choo-choo-choo-choo
Choo-choo-choo-choo

2

I would pull the horn...

7

The engineer is operating the locomotive and the train is moving fast.

4

Watch the cars go by—
the caboose is near the last.

5

Train Pattern

Locomotive

Teacher Directions: Copy the pattern onto white construction paper. Use with pages 75 and 76.

Directions

1. Color the pattern.

2. Cut out the pattern.

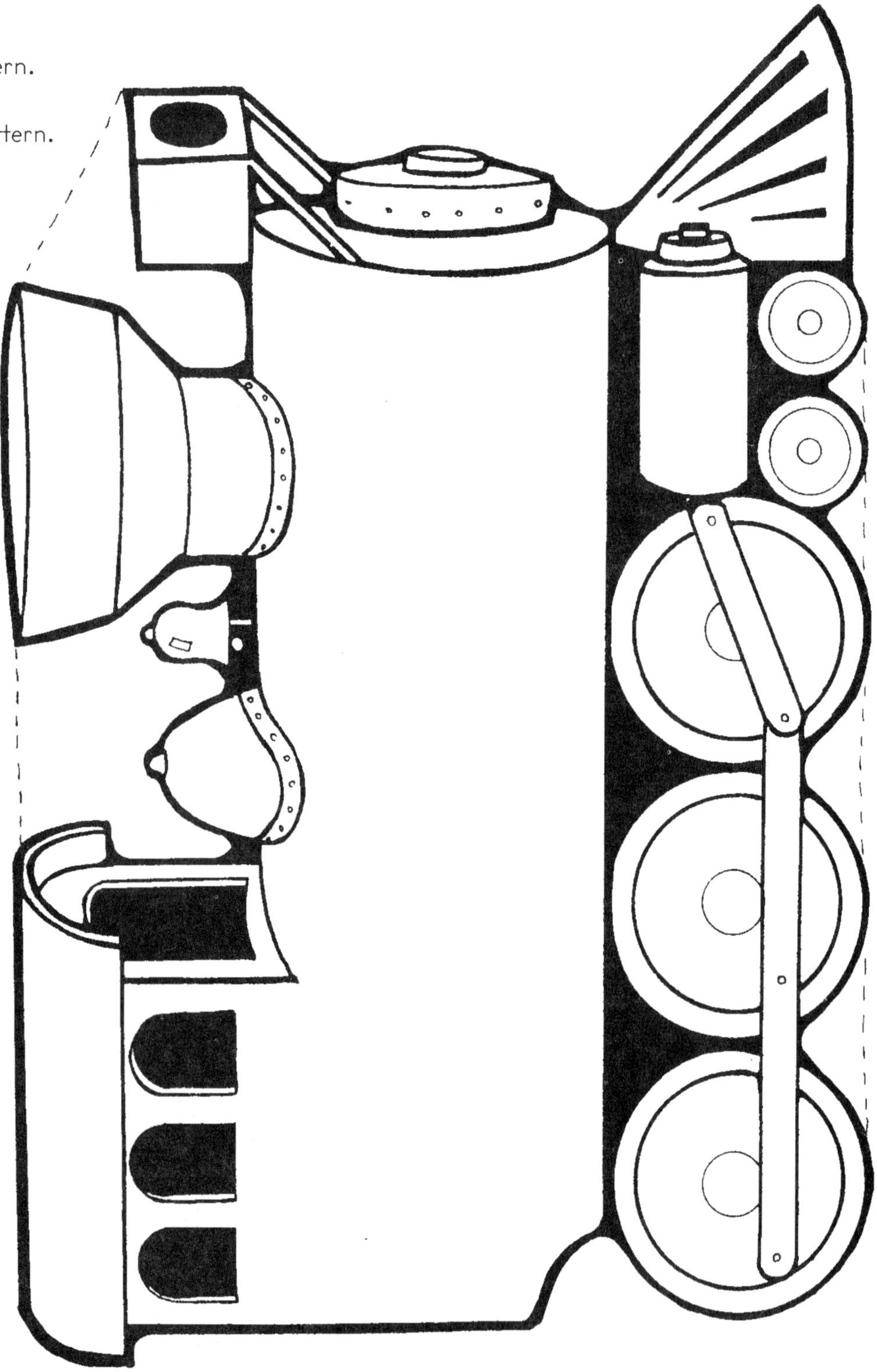

Train Pattern

Train Car

Teacher Directions: Copy the pattern onto white construction paper. Use with pages 74 and 76.

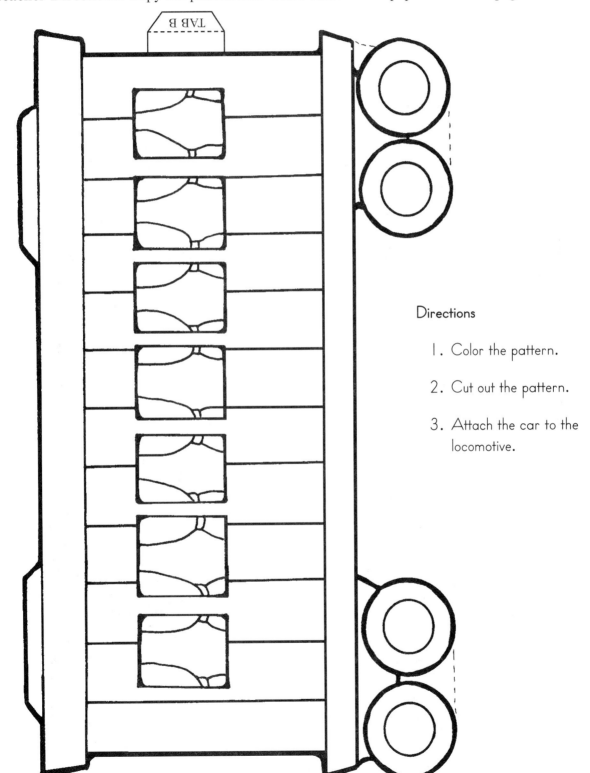

Directions

1. Color the pattern.

2. Cut out the pattern.

3. Attach the car to the locomotive.

Train Pattern

Caboose

Teacher Directions: Copy the pattern onto white construction paper. Use with pages 74 and 75.

Directions

1. Color the caboose red.

2. Cut out the pattern.

3. Attach the caboose to the car.

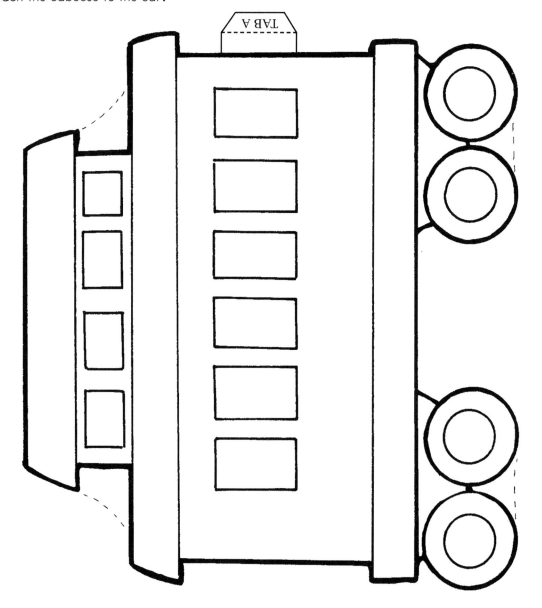

There are so many choices.
Which would you choose?

8

Boats

Some are at play.

6

little boats

3

Big boats and

2

Barges and jet skis, tug boats and canoes...

7

all over the place.

4

Some are at work.

5

Boat Pattern

Sail

Teacher Directions: Copy the pattern onto white construction paper. Use with page 80.

Directions

   1. Paint or color the sails.

   2. Cut out the pattern.

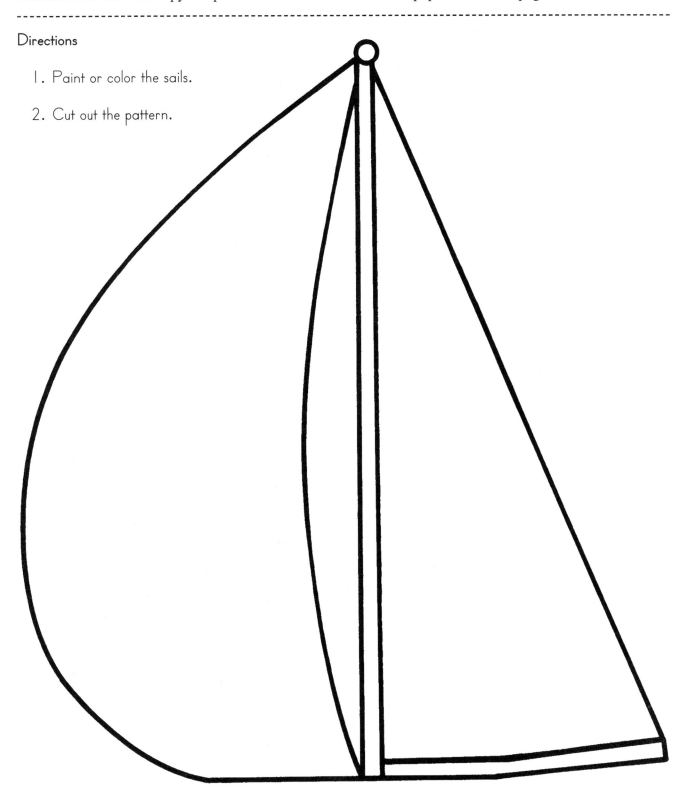

Boat Pattern

Boat Hull

Teacher Directions: Copy the pattern onto white construction paper. Use with page 79.

Directions

1. Color the pattern.

2. Cut out the pattern.

3. Attach the boat to the sails.

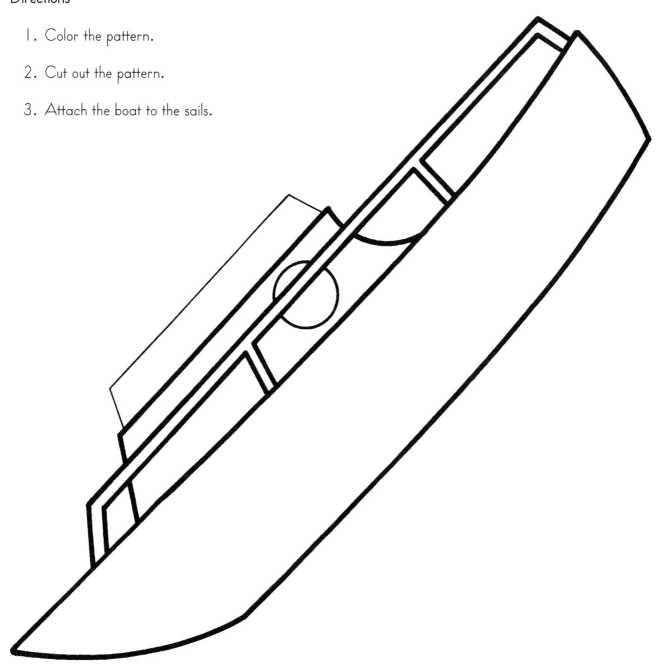

and maybe bring them home.

8

Space Travel

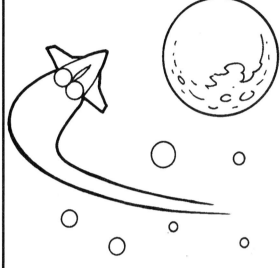

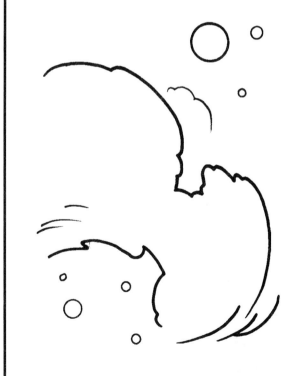

into the dark unknown—

6

out of sight.

3

I want to get in a rocket and be bolted...

2

and someday meet some aliens...

7

I want to fly up to the moon just like an astronaut.

4

I want to soar right through the stars—

5

Space Travel Pattern

Rocket

Teacher Directions: Copy the pattern onto white construction paper. Use with page 84.

Directions

1. Paint the rocket, using watercolors.

2. Cut out the pattern.

Space Travel Pattern

Rocket Top and Fire

Teacher Directions: Copy the pattern onto white construction paper. If possible, offer red and yellow cellophane to make additional flames at the base of the rocket. Use with page 83.

Directions

1. Tear construction paper into pieces and glue them to the top pattern.

2. Color the fire, using red, yellow and orange crayons.

3. Cut out the patterns.

4. Glue the top pattern to the rocket top. (Have the overlap show in the front.)

5. Glue the fire to the back of the rocket bottom.

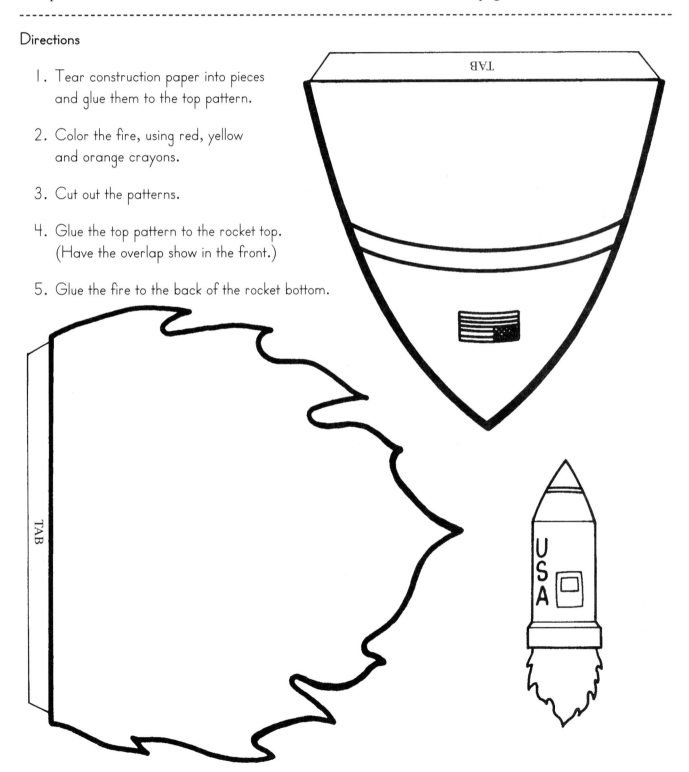

Canada Fun

Canada Facts

- Canada is the second largest country in land size in the world.
- Ottawa is Canada's capital.
- Canada is the country north of the United States. Canada has more land and the United States has more people.
- Canada's flag is red and white with a red maple leaf in the center.
- The maple leaf is the most recognized symbol of Canada.
- The beaver is a national symbol for Canada. It represents authority.
- Canada's national police force is called the Royal Canadian Mounted Police or Mounties.
- The longest paved road in the world is located in Canada. It is called the Trans-Canada Highway.
- Niagara Falls is located in Ontario, Canada. It is one of the natural wonders of the world.
- Canada is one of the world's largest producers of wheat. Beef cattle, spruce and pine trees, and petroleum are other important products.
- French and English are the two official languages in Canada.
- Canada Day is a national holiday and falls on July 1st.

Canada Fun Activities

1. Locate Canada on a globe. What oceans border it?
2. Measure the number of miles from your hometown to Ottawa.
3. Identify the different modes of transportation to travel to Canada.
4. Try maple syrup on various foods.
5. Start an e-pal correspondence with a class from Canada.
6. Learn how to say hello in French—"bon-jour."

Book List

Kalman, Bobbie. *Canada A to Z.* Crabtree Publishing Company, 1999.

Kalman, Bobbie. *Canada: The Culture.* Crabtree Publishing Company, 1993.

Kalman, Bobbie. *Canada: The People.* Crabtree Publishing Company, 1993.

Canada Sites

http://www.imagesoft.net/canada/can-symb.html
Do you know the symbols of Canada? Check out this site to learn more about the Canadian flag, the maple leaf, and the beaver.

http://www.craigmarlatt.com/craig/canada
Find out about the symbols of Canada and much more.

http://www.enchantedlearning.com/school/canada
Learn about the Canadian culture at Enchanted Learning.

French and English are spoken in Canada.

8

Canada

The beaver is a symbol of Canada.

6

Ottawa is the capital of Canada.

3

This is Canada.

2

Some police officers in Canada are called "mounties."

7

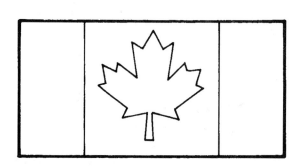

This is the Canadian flag. A red maple leaf is in the center.

4

Canada's national tree is the maple.

5

Canada Pattern

Canadian Flag

Teacher Directions: Copy the pattern onto white construction paper.

Directions

Color the maple leaf and the two side panels red.

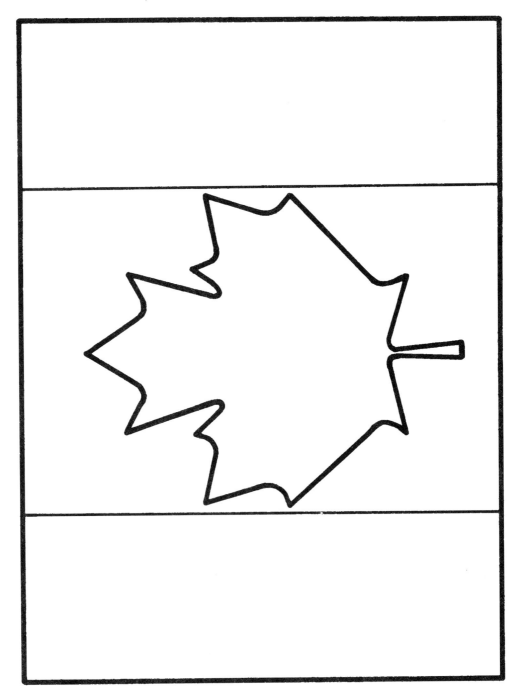

Canada Pattern

Beaver Head

Teacher Directions: Copy the pattern onto white construction paper. Each child needs a paper headband. Use with page 90.

- -

Directions

1. Trace the lines using a black crayon.

2. Paint over the pattern using brown watercolor.

3. Cut out the pattern.

4. Glue the beaver head to the front of a paper headband.

Canada Pattern

Beaver Tail

Teacher Directions: Copy the pattern onto white construction paper. Use with page 89.

- -

Directions

1. Trace the lines using a black crayon.

2. Color the tail pattern brown.

3. Cut out the pattern.

4. Attach the tail to the back of the paper headband.

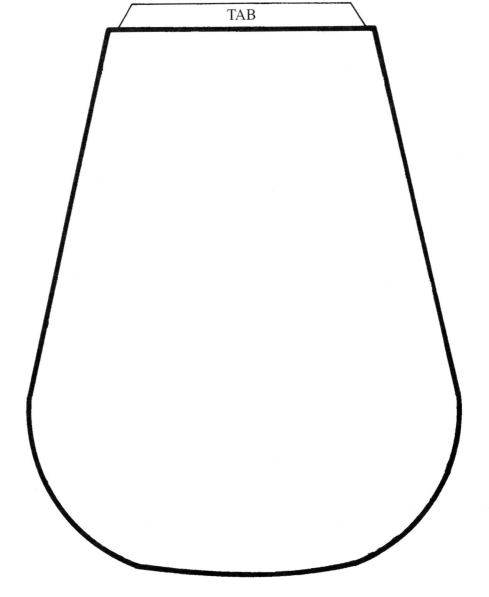

TAB

Mexico Fun

Mexico Facts

- Mexico is a country located south of the United States.
- The official language of Mexico is Spanish.
- Mexico's flag is green, white and red with a coat of arms in the center.
- Mexico is known for its beautiful beaches and its Aztec and Mayan ruins.
- The capital and largest city of Mexico is Mexico City.
- A Mexican celebration is called a "fiesta."
- A custom in Mexico is to take a "siesta" between the hours of 2 and 5 each day. A siesta is a nap.
- Corn (maiz) is an important crop in Mexico. Many foods in Mexico are made from corn including tortillas, burritos, and quesadillas.
- Mexico is known for its ceramics and its murals.
- Soccer is the most important sport in Mexico. Baseball, jai alai, and bullfights are also important.

Mexico Fun Activities

1. Locate Mexico on a globe. Measure how far it is from the school or your home.
2. Have the children break a piñata.
3. Have a class fiesta. Dance, paint a mural, or have a soccer game. Include Latin music and foods from Mexico.
4. Make pottery using modeling clay. Decorate it using Aztec or Mayan symbols.

Book List

Arnold, Helen. *Post Cards From Mexico.* Raintree Steck-Vaughn, 1996.

Bulmer-Thomas, Barbara. *Journey Through Mexico.* Troll Associates, 1991.

Haskins, Jim. *Count Your Way Through Mexico.* Carolrhoda Books, Inc., 1989.

Jacobsen, Karen. *Mexico.* Children's Press, 1984.

Kalmen, Bobbie. *Mexico from A to Z.* Crabtree Publishing, 1999.

Mexico Sites

http://www.elbalero.gob.mx/index_kids.html
Explore the Mexican culture, listen to authentic Mexican music and find recipes of Mexican dishes at this site.

http://home.earthlink.net/~mikcar
Learn how to speak Spanish! This site has an audio and visual format.

http://www.atozkidsstuff.com/mexico.html
This is a great site for facts about Mexico.

What is your favorite Mexican food?

8

Mexico has beautiful beaches.

6

This is Mexico's flag. The coat of arms is in the center.

3

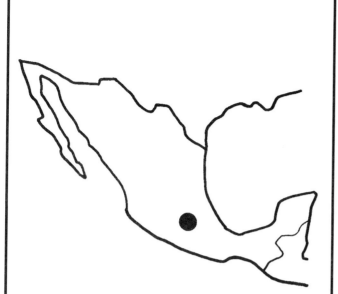

This is Mexico. Its capital is Mexico City.

2

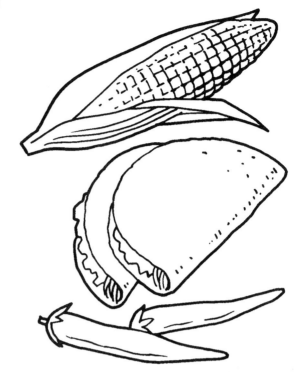

Many people like Mexican food.

7

In Mexico, parties are called fiestas. There is music and dancing.

4

¡HOLA!

Spanish is the language of Mexico.

5

Mexico Pattern

Mexican Flag

Teacher Directions: Copy the pattern onto white construction paper.

- -

Directions

1. Color the stripe on the left green.

2. Color the stripe on the right red.

3. Color the coat of arms.

4. Cut out the flag.

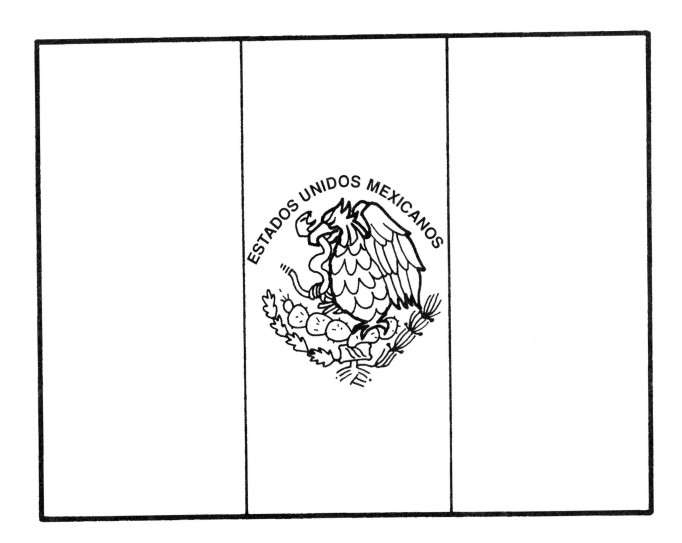

Mexico Pattern

Mexican Piñata

Teacher Directions: Copy the pattern onto white construction paper. Provide tissue paper in a variety of colors.

Directions

1. Color the pattern.

2. Cut out the pattern and decorate it with torn pieces of tissue paper.

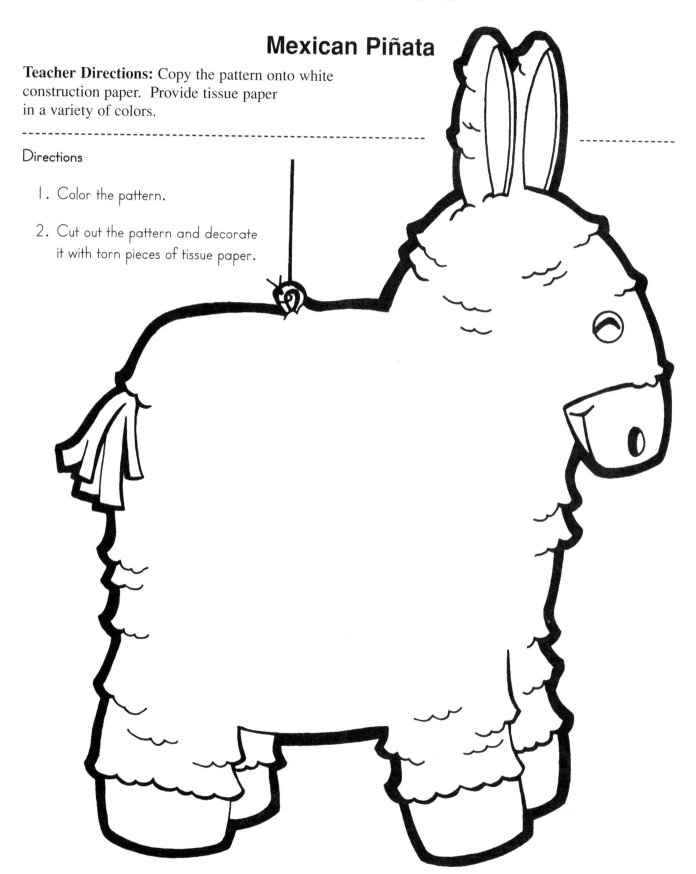

United States of America Fun

Untied States of America Facts

- The capital of the United States is Washington, D.C.
- The President lives in the White House, which is located in Washington, D.C.
- The USA is the fourth largest country in land mass in the world.
- The American flag is red, white, and blue with 50 stars and 13 stripes.
- The stripes on the flag represent the first 13 colonies.
- The 50 stars represent the 50 states in America.
- The National Anthem is the "Star Spangled Banner."
- The national bird is the bald eagle. It represents strength and power.
- The Statue of Liberty is located in New York. It stands for freedom and was a gift from France. It stands 152 feet tall.
- The USA was the first country in the world to send an astronaut to the moon.

United States of America Fun Activities

1. Locate the United States of America on the globe.
2. Identify the distance from your town to Washington, D.C.
3. Draw a flag. Try to include 13 stripes and all 50 stars.
4. Have a red, white and blue tasting party. Ask parents to send food representing those colors (juices, blueberries, red or blue jello, apples, etc.).
5. Baseball is known as a national past time in the United States. Have a class baseball game.

Book List

Kalman, Bobbie. *The United States from A to Z.* Crabtree Publishing Co., 1999.

Keller, Laurie. *The Scrambled States of America.* Henry Holt & Company, Inc., 2000.

Loomis, Christine. *Across America, I Love You.* Hyperion Press, 2000.

United States of America Sites

http://www.pbs.org/democracy/kids
Find out what it would be like to be the President of the United States of America. Answer a few simple questions and you "become" president for a day.

http://www.usflag.org
Learn about the history of the flag and the words to the pledge.

http://bensguide.gpo.gov
Ben's Guide is an excellent site to find information about the government and symbols of the United States. This site is divided into grade levels.

The Statue of Liberty is a symbol of America.

8

United States of America

The bald eagle is a symbol of America.

6

Washington, D.C. is the capital of the U.S.A.

3

This is the United States of America.

2

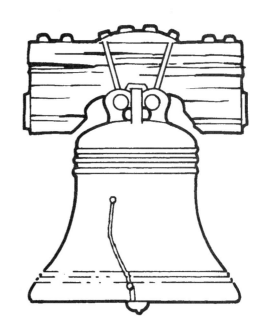

The Liberty Bell is a symbol of America.

7

This is the American flag.

4

It has 50 stars. It has 13 stripes.

5

United States of America Pattern

USA Flag

Teacher Directions: Copy the pattern onto white construction paper.

Directions

1. Color the stripes red and white.

2. Color the background to the stars blue.

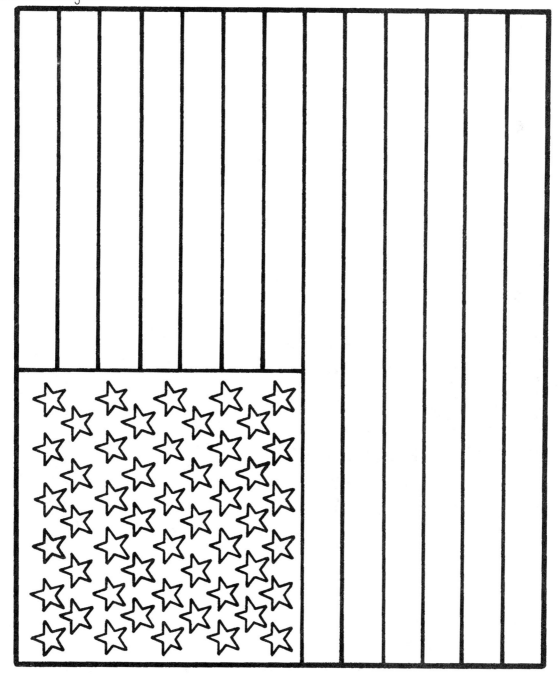

United States of America Pattern

Statue of Liberty

Teacher Directions: Copy the pattern onto white construction paper. Use with page 101.

Directions

1. Use a green crayon to trace the lines on the pattern.

2. Paint the pattern using green watercolor.

United States of America Pattern

Statue of Liberty Base

Teacher Directions: Copy the pattern onto white construction paper. Use with page 100.

- -

Directions

1. Use a green crayon to trace the lines on the pattern.

2. Paint the pattern using green watercolor.

3. Attach the base to the statue at the tab.

United States of America Pattern

Eagle

Teacher Directions: Copy the pattern onto white construction paper.

Directions

1. Color the eagle's wings and body brown.
2. Color the claws and beak yellow.
3. Tear white construction paper into pieces. (Glue pieces to cover the eagle's head.)

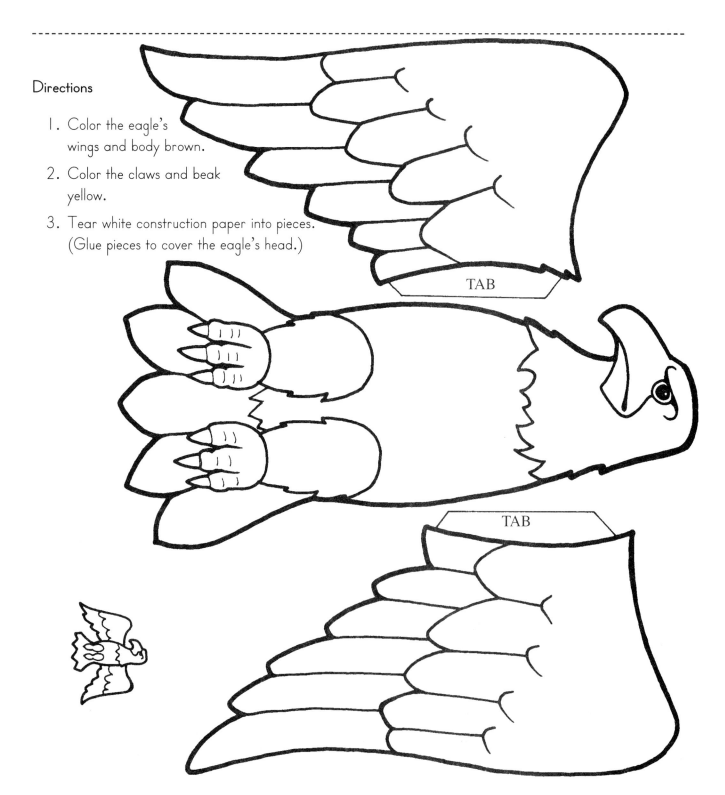

United States of America Pattern

Liberty Bell

Teacher Directions: Copy the patterns onto white construction paper. Use with page 104.

Directions

1. Use a black crayon to trace the pattern lines.

2. Paint the pattern using black or gray watercolor.

3. Cut out the pattern.

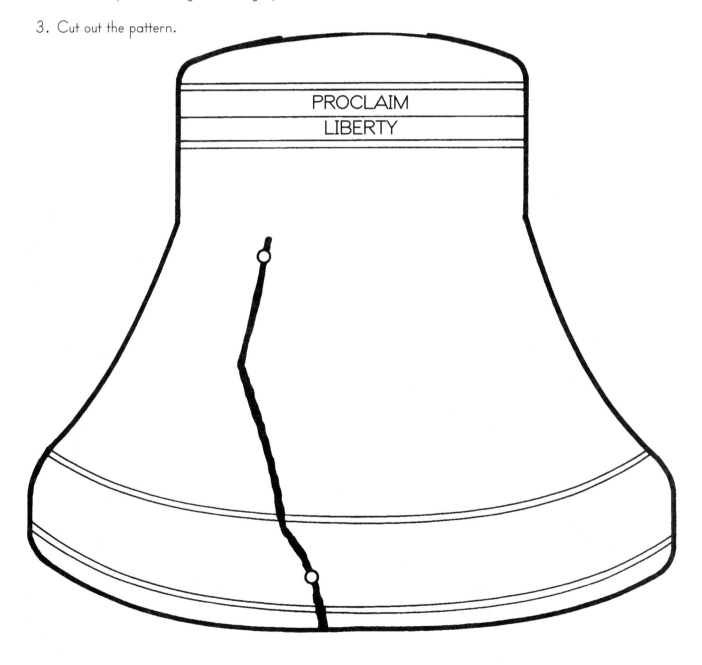

PROCLAIM
LIBERTY

United States of America Pattern

Liberty Bell Top

Teacher Directions: Copy the patterns onto white construction paper. Use with page 103.

Directions

1. Tear brown construction paper in to small pieces.

2. Cover the base of the Liberty Bell with the torn pieces.

3. Cut out the pattern.

4. Attach the bell to the base at the tab.

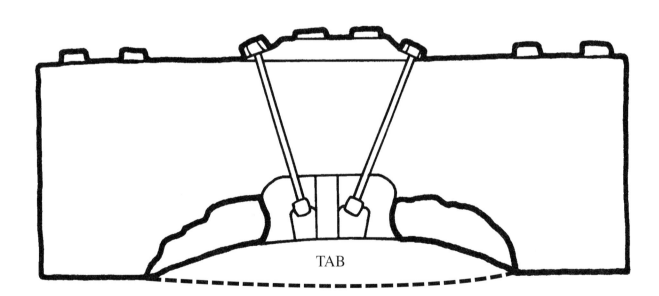

TAB

Communication Fun

Communication Facts

- Communication is the passing of information.
- There are many ways to communicate.
- One way people communicate is through speech, body language and sign language.
- Early inventions began opening doors for global communication.
- The printing press was invented by Johannes Gutenburg in the early 1450's.
- The first telephone was invented by Alexander Graham Bell in 1876.
- The first typewriter was invented by Christopher Latham Sholes in 1898.
- The first radio transmission was by Guglielmo Marconi in 1901.
- The first television was invented by Philo Farmsworth in 1927.
- The first computer was invented in 1945.
- The Internet was invented in 1973.

Communication Fun Activities

1. Visit the local television and radio stations, telephone company and newspaper office.
2. Find an e-pal from another country.
3. Draw a picture of a futuristic means of communication.
4. Discuss the time involved with the transmission/receiving of information through different means—snail mail, e-mail, telephone, etc.
5. Discuss telephone and Internet etiquette.
6. Find out how people communicated before cars and planes were invented.

Book List

Ganeri, Anita. *The Story of Communications*. Oxford University Press Childrens Books, 1998.

Grimshaw, Caroline. *Communication*. World Book of Encyclopedia, 1998.

Pollard, Michael. *Alexander Graham Bell: Father of Modern Communication*. Blackbirch Marketing, 2000.

Communication Websites

http://www.inventorsmuseum.com/comm.htm
Visit the Inventors Museum and discover when various communication devices were invented.

http://cbc4kids.ca/general/the-lab/history-of-invention
Explore the time line of inventions! Find out interesting facts about the telephone, television and computers.

http://www.enchantedlearning.com/inventors/communication
Learn about the inventors of various communication devices from the fountain pen to the television.

How Do We Communicate?

How will we communicate in the future?

8

How do we communicate?

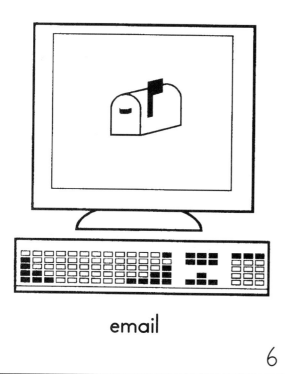

email

6

How do we communicate?

snail mail

3

How do we communicate?

newspaper

2

How do we communicate?

cellular phones

7

How do we communicate?

telephone

4

How do we communicate?

television

5

Communication Pattern

World

Teacher Directions: Copy the pattern onto white construction paper. Each child needs 4–6 inch pieces of yarn. Use with page 109.

Directions

1. Color the land areas green.

2. Paint the water areas blue using watercolor.

3. Cut out the pattern.

Communication Pattern

Communication Devices

Teacher Directions: Copy the pattern onto white construction paper. Use with page 108.

Directions

1. Color and cut out the patterns.

2. Tape the yarn to the back of each pattern.

3. Tape the other end of the yarn to the back of the world pattern.

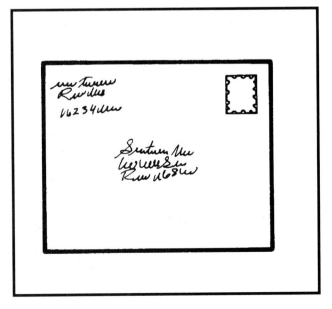

Land and Water Fun

Land and Water Facts

- The planet Earth is made up of land and water.

- Some land is high. A mountain is the highest form of land. A hill is not as high as a mountain.

- Some land is flat. A plain is mostly flat land.

- People use land in many ways (farming, play, homes, etc.).

- Streams, rivers, lakes and oceans are bodies of water.

- An ocean is the largest body of water. Ocean water is salty.

- A river is a long body of water that flows to an ocean.

- A lake is a large body of water that is surrounded by land.

- People use water in many ways (fishing, drinking, swimming, etc.).

Land and Water Fun Activities

1. Identify different landforms and bodies of water near your town.

2. Visit some local land and water sites.

3. Draw a picture and write about personal experience with mountains, oceans, etc.

4. Make lists of your favorite things to do on land and water.

Book List

Dorros, Arthur. *Follow the Water from Brook to Ocean.* HarperTrophy, 1993.

Hale, Wendy. *The Florida Water Story: From Raindrops to the Sea.* Pineapple Press, 1998.

Zoehfeld, Kathleen. *How Mountains are Made.* HarperTrophy, 1995.

Land and Water Websites

http://www.ccsd.k12.wy.us/Social%20Studies/06/0205landforms.html
Investigate the different landforms: continents, mountains, plains, islands and other landforms.

http://mbgnet.mobot.org
Learn about the different landforms and water systems of the world.

http://www.athena.ivv.nasa.gov/curric/land/landform/landform.html
This site is loaded with graphics and information about different landforms.

People need the land and the
water.

8

Land and Water

A river is a body of water.

6

Some land is high—hills and
mountains.

3

The earth has land and water.

2

An ocean is a body of water.

7

Some land is flat
—plains and grasslands.

4

A lake is a body of water.

5

Land and Water Pattern

Our World

Teacher Directions: Copy the pattern onto white construction paper.

- -

Directions

1. Color the land areas with a dark green crayon.

2. Paint the water areas blue using watercolor.

3. Draw your favorite thing to do on land and in the water. Use the boxes provided.

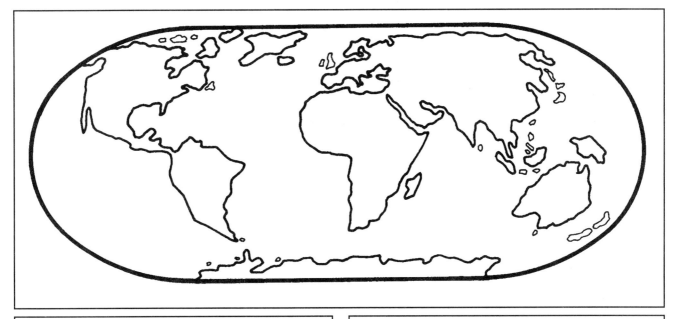

Land	Water

Natural Resources Fun

Natural Resources Facts

- Trees, soil, oil, gas, water, etc., are natural resources. Natural resources are something people use to meet their needs.
- People use trees for food, building materials and paper goods.
- People use soil to grow plants and trees.
- People use oil and gas to heat their homes, cook, and for fuel.
- People use water to drink, bathe, cook, etc.
- It is important that people take care of our natural resources.
- Recycling, reducing and reusing help to take care of natural resources.
- Controlling pollution is another way to take care of natural resources.
- Pollution is the contamination of the air, water or soil.

Natural Resources Fun Activities

1. List the many ways people use trees, water, etc.
2. Plant a tree at school or at home.
3. Set up a recycling center at your school or at home.
4. Invite a conservationist to talk about the importance of saving natural resources.
5. Use recycled items to make creative art projects.

Book List

Kalman, Bobbie. *Natural Resources*. Crabtree Publishing, 1987.

Lauber, Patricia. *Be a Friend to Trees*. HarperCollins Juvenile Books, 1996.

Parker, Steve. *Earth's Resources*. Raintree/Steck-Vaughn, 2001.

Silverstein, Shel. *The Giving Tree*. HarperCollins Juvenile Books, 1986.

Natural Resources Websites

http://www.dnr.state.sc.us/etc/education.html
South Carolina's Natural Resource site provides helpful ways to involve children in the protection and conservation of natural resources.

http://www.recycleworks.org/kids/index.html
Learn the process of recycle, reuse and reduce.

http://www.epa.gov/kids/osw_kids_page.htm
Join the planet protectors club and lean how to save our natural resources.

http://www.epa.gov/kids/garbage.htm
Find out how to protect our water systems, plants, air and animals.

Love the Earth...

Help take care of me!

8

Natural Resources: Water

and drinking water

6

I am a natural resource.

3

I am water.

2

and water for cleaning.

7

I give people many things.

4

I give food

5

Love the Earth.

Plant a tree!

8

Natural Resources: Trees

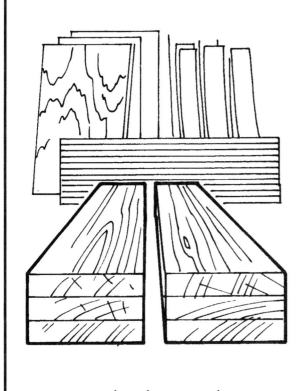

lumber and

6

I am a natural resource.

3

I am a tree.

2

...paper.

7

I give people many things.

4

I give fruit and

5

Natural Resources Pattern

Tree Top

Teacher Directions: Copy the pattern onto white construction paper. Use with pages 120, 121 and 122.

- -

Directions

1. Tear green paper into pieces and glue them on the pattern.

2. Cut out the pattern.

Natural Resources Pattern

Tree Trunk

Teacher Directions: Copy the pattern onto white construction paper. Use with pages 119, 121 and 122.

- -

Directions

1. Use a black crayon to trace the lines of the pattern.

2. Paint the trunk using brown watercolor.

3. Cut out the pattern.

4. Attach to the tree's top.

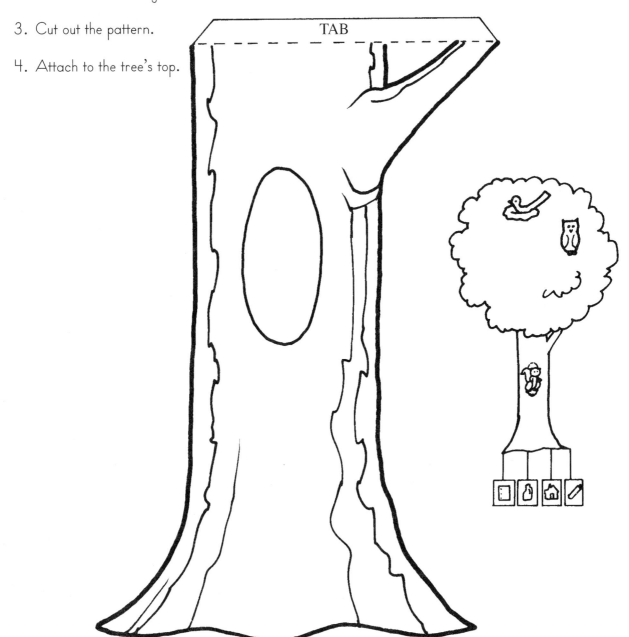

Natural Resources Pattern

Wood Products

Teacher Directions: Copy the pattern onto white construction paper. Each child needs four 6 inch pieces of yarn. Use with pages 119, 120 and 122.

- -

Directions

1. Color and cut out the patterns.

2. Tape yarn to the back of the patterns.

3. Tape the other end of the yarn to the back of the tree.

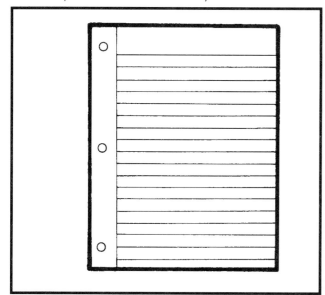

Natural Resources Pattern

Tree Animals

Teacher Directions: Copy the pattern onto white construction paper. Use with pages 119, 120 and 121.

- -

Directions

   1. Color the patterns.

   2. Cut out the patterns.

   3. Glue the patterns to the tree.

I Know About Family

I Know About Different Homes

I Know About School

I Know About Community Helpers

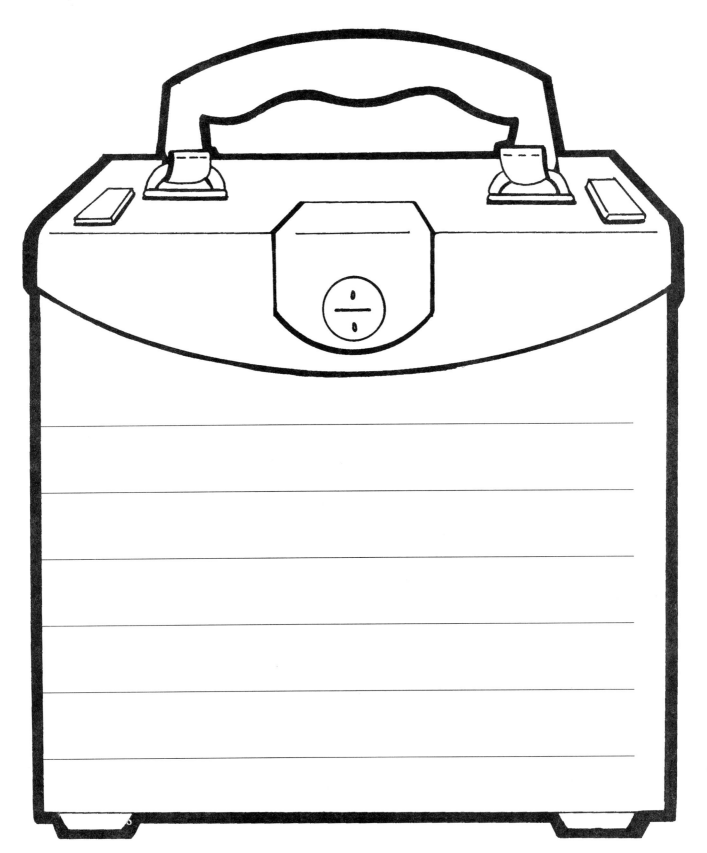

I Know About the Post Office

I Know About the Hospital

Rx

I Know About the Bank

$ Bank $

I Know About Police Officers

POLICE

I Know About Fire Fighters

I Know About Producers

I Know About Consumers

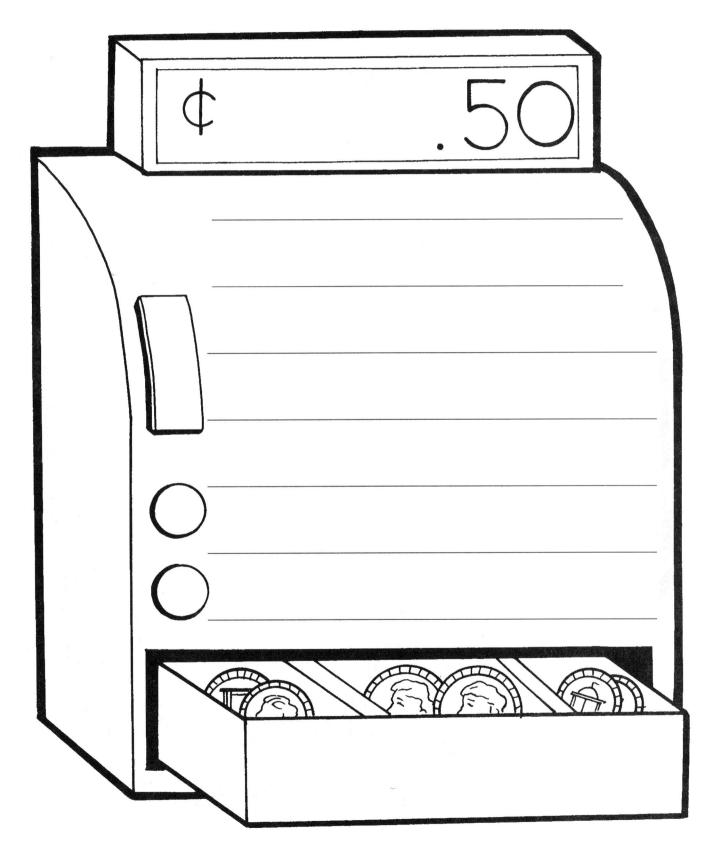

I Know About Aircraft

I Know About Cars and Trucks

I Know About Trains

I Know About Boats

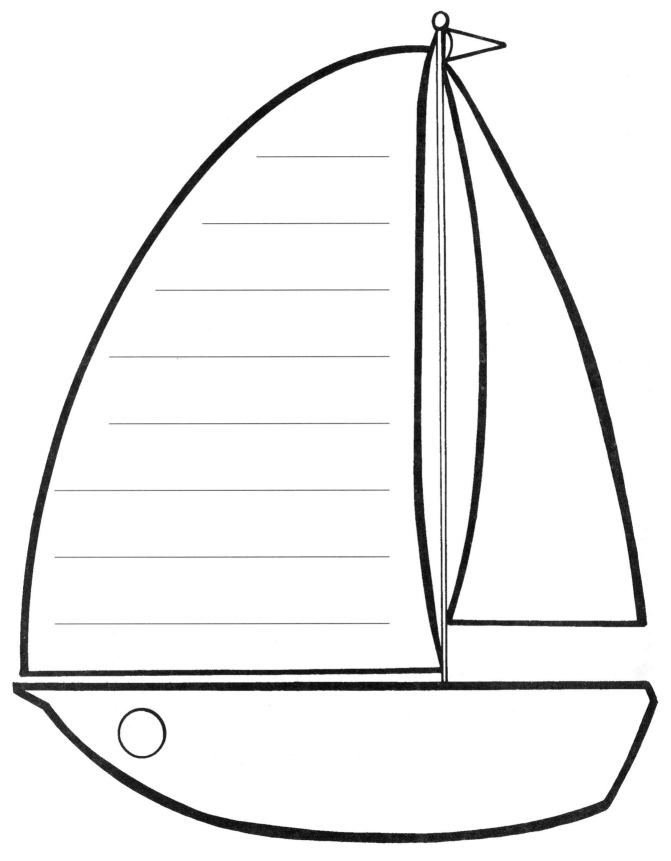

I Know About Spacecraft

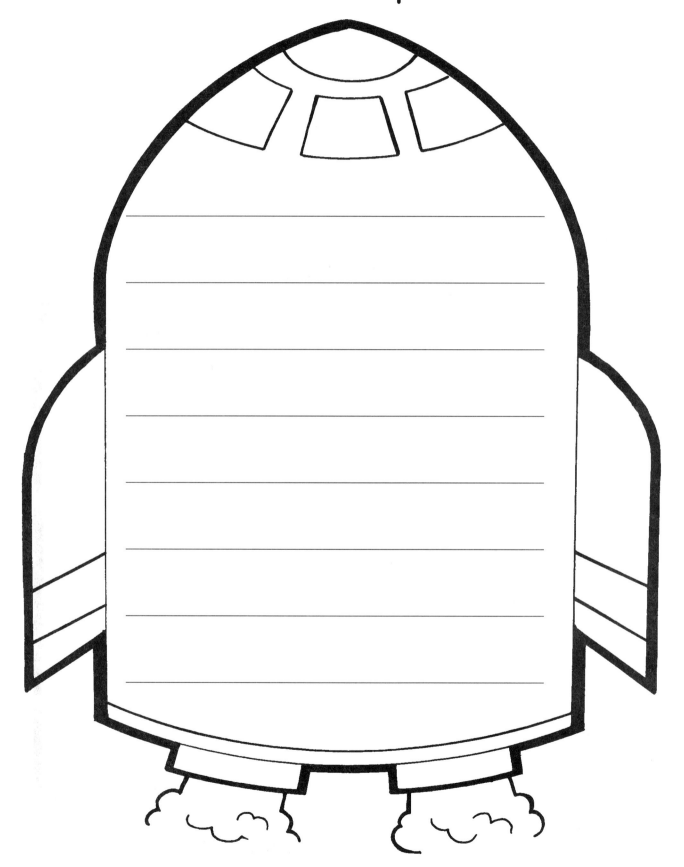

I Know About Canada

Maple Syrup

I Know About Mexico

I Know About the United States of America

I Know About Communication

I Know About Land and Water

I Know About Natural Resources